THE LARGE EBOR COLLIDER

York Poetry Workshop accelerates the imagination, colliding here and there to generate poetronic particles

A collection of the poetry featured in York Poetry Workshop's performance at York Literature Festival 2014

Featuring poems by:

John Atkinson

Frank Broughton

Phil Connolly

Debbie Jayne Howell

Jamie Howell

Margaret Speak

Charles Tomson

Peter R White

Peter Wright

Edited by Peter R White
With an introduction by Margaret Speak

Published 2014 by
Whitelight Press, 6 Oakdale Meadow, Leeds, LS14 2HB, UK

Cover illustration: adapted from *Ammortality* by Peter R White

ISBN 978-0-9927616-1-5

Printed by
imprintdigital.com, Seychelles Farm, Upton Pyne. Devon. EX5 5YX
info@imprintdigital.com

Contents

Foreword

When York Poetry Workshop were invited to stage an event at the York Literature Festival 2014, we decided that, rather than follow the usual route of having a succession of poets, each reading for ten minutes or so, we should provide a mixture of voices and styles, interspersed with a few snippets of music to lighten up the proceedings. I carelessly volunteered to look at the possibility of grouping poems together into themed sets and found myself bombarded by and subsequently absorbed in reading a swathe of wonderful poetry, from which I soon identified numerous common topics and themes. I set up an Excel spreadsheet (as we nerdy types are inclined to do), which enabled me to move the listed poems around into groups having common themes and soon realised I was pulling together a lively and diverse set of opinions, rather like the conversations we have in the pub after our monthly Saturday morning workshops.

The next task was to prune the list into a series of small sets or *scenes* and then prune further to make sure that the final collection would not overrun the time allocated for our theatre production. The result is arguably not a collection of the 'best' poetry we as a group could have created – there were so many of our favourite poems 'on the cutting room floor'. Nevertheless, after I had circulated the draft *script* to the members, the mutual opinion was that it was worthy of more than a single theatrical performance. So we investigated the possibility of publishing an anthology, which turned out to be affordable, and so here it is all the words from the script of our performance at the Friargate Theatre, York on Sunday 23rd March 2014.

The intention is to have copies on sale at the performance and, at the time of writing, we have not got round to making plans for additional marketing. I wonder how you came by this copy.

Peter R White

Introduction

York Poetry Workshop was founded in the nineteen sixties by Sir Herbert Read, artist, poet and critic. It was started in an abandoned church on Micklegate, which had become an Arts Centre. Sir Herbert decided that as there was no money in poetry but it was an important art form it should have a kind of protected status. The Workshop ran there happily for many years until the Arts Centre closed. It is reputed to be the oldest continuing poetry workshop in the country. Now we meet informally once a month on a Saturday morning, which seems fortuitous as after the meeting we retire to the pub where the debate and craic continue. We try to uphold the tradition of good contemporary writing with fierce debate and discussion and occasional prizes and publication. All are welcome to attend.

I love the notion of the Hadron Collider as suggested by Peter Wright having now become the Ebor Collider in deference to York. Here we have a confluence of words, themes and ideas with unpredictable results. The main themes seem to be Nature, Place, History, Intrigue, Love, Life and Death. So no surprises there then!

But there may be.

Margaret Speak
Chair, York Poetry Workshop

Scene 1: Time

Peter R White
Nursery Chime

Adagio, we hear the pulse of night...
whispering trees that wave... to... fro...
a sibilant two-step seduced by a fickle breeze...
a chord diminished to a single string
diminuendo... the owl who hoots alone.
Beads of frozen dew gleam on the lawn
beneath a waxing quarter moon that glints
on hints of frost that form on leaded windows.

Inside the house a solitary shaft
of moonbeam through the shutters concentrates
a line across a floor of solid oak:
pale light diffused by beads of settled breath
and lingering aromas of a cup
of cocoa carried up those stairs that creaked
when dancing shadows flickered lightly up
into the gentle land of sleep.

A mist has littered crisp haphazard shapes
since whiffs of chocolate and burnt candle wax
have left their scents, which now condense like crystal
waves on frosted glass. The moments pass
as, beat by steady beat, the clock repeats
its tut... its tut... its tut... (no tock we hear).
Its northern, glottal stop locates its voice:
its tut... its tut... Its tut... its tut... its tut...
in steady plod towards the smallest hour.

1

John Harrison made every piece by hand:
the frame, the wheels and outer case from oak;
while boxwood forms the spindles and the pinions;
the pendulum is dark mahogany
(not hickory). His dad taught John his craft:
showed how to make it pace a steady beat
to keep a constant sixty to the minute –
each movement eased by rubbing beeswax in it.

But now we hear a pittery-pattery-pit
in syncopation with its tut... its tut...
its tut... its tut... its pittery-pattery-pit
moves up inside the hard oak frame.
And in the dark the house is unaware;
the strip of light that sidles near the stair
ignores the sound as, one inch at a time,
a tiny creature scrapes and scratches up
until at last, when it gets to the top,
the mouse sniffs for the sweet aroma of
the beeswax polished into boxwood bits
that regulate its tut... its tut... its tut...
and liberate the tension on the spring
that lifts the hammer from the gong, to drop
and generate a solitary BONG... ng...

The shattered silence hears a scittery-scat
as tiny claws descend at rapid pace
and scrape and scamper back across the floor.
A flick disturbs the shaft of waxen light
that withers as a cloud decides to shroud

the moon and fill the room with blackness,
while the clock retains its tut... its tut...
outweighs the mouse's palpitating heart
that hurries through the draught beneath the door
to interrupt the gentle pulse of night
and leave the darkened house with nothing but
its tut... its tut... its tut... its tut... its tut...

John Atkinson
The Memory of Trees

Churchyard yews shroud the dead,
weep at the mention of Crecy
or Agincourt. Great oaks quake
recalling Henry's navy. A lone elm
assumes the role of Last of the Mohicans.
Ash and chestnut await the inevitable.

Overhead, leaves sway on waves of wind.
Beneath the canopy time flows
in shades of green. Bark encircles whims
of bygone seasons, ring by spreading ring.
Under the quiet wood
roots communicate.

Iron, bronze, stone: the old forest falls,
dwellings rise, sparks soar
into darkening skies, roasting meat spits;
tonight the tribe will not go hungry.
Millennia they stood,
waiting to warm us.

Peter Wright
Baille Hill *

Even in summer the steps stay wet
blackened by thousands of rotted leaves
from cloak of sycamore and beneath,
shoots of lost elms fighting to set
their colours in the light; waves
of contest, stains of death.

Thrown up in ten sixty-nine
by command of William, this motte,
white with umbels of cow parsley, tall
fetid hemlock, remains malign,
high, strangely unfrequented, not
crowned with castellated wall.

Below, now-fashionable terraces
glow with good taste: muted colours,
authentic door-furniture, floral displays;
but through the gloom as daylight passes
see the blue flicker of computers,
ghost embers of a long-extinguished blaze.

* Built in York in the year in which King William launched his Harrying Of The
North: "Leave no living thing between York and Durham."

Frank Broughton
St Fillan's Cure

If you are sick in mind or heart
then go, according to your kind,
to the Pool of Women or the Pool
of Men, step down and slowly sink
into the clear water of St Fillan's
stream but do not drink, instead
pick up nine pebbles from its stony bed
then circle three times round
the triple cairns beside that spot
and each time drop one stone,
then drape a scarf or place a bonnet
on the largest pile and leave the pools
behind, walk barefoot back until you come
to where the saint is sleeping under slabs,
lie down and let yourself be tightly
bound with ropes to Fillan's rack,
your head supported by the crumbling
font and fitted with a holy cap of bronze,
the Bennane Bell, that in times gone
called the glen's faithful, tolled its dead.
Now must your friends lay over you
a mantle of clean hay then leave
you to the night and stars until at light
of day they find you loosed and healed,
if not, repeat the ritual, but should you feel
this is too much to bear then sit down
on the bank beside the pools and listen
to the song of birds, observe the shadow

play of Fillan's trout, and watch Ben Lui's
winter snows transmute from grey
to gold along its eastward flank, breathe
deep of mountain air and be content.

Jamie Howell
Rackwick

I looked over to Rackwick Bay
saw the stones of Hoy grey in the mist,
caressed into place as a comfort in a storm.

Cold graveyard granite touched and slow moan
cries in the dawn's refrain of Solstice bells sang
war liturgies lining the Sound.

Pride laments in rumours of violence lost;
merely a harvest of men amongst the clearances
of the past and future postscripts in the present.

There were no dreams left; with all pomp we bore them
away in circumstances that scree'd and screamed
a thousand thousand tides lining time: funeral processions.

Weak sun cuts the grey, shines on memories to come;
memorial whispers seeking loved ones
who must go home.

Debbie Jayne Howell

Saturday

Today is Saturday and the sunny room where I write
has wooden floorboards and spiky clocks
all stopped at different times;
the hand winding them having died.
The other room has mirrors of all shapes and sizes
misshapen rough or hewn glass shrunk to a manageable
    glance.
There is a picture on the wall of a Thai woman
rich in yellow red pattern;
a reminder of my grandfather in another room
where his old wooden mirror hung
on a chain as if he wasn't dead.
My grandmother winds the finger orange gold clock,
steps back with a chuckle to argue some long remembered
    debate
as we sit around the table of fractured memory.

Peter R White
Always

Whenever a red kite glides by
the silver birch you planted,
high against a summer sky above
the field where pale blue flax once grew,
when it splays dark fingers, sways
its forked tail lazily to switch
its drift, I'll remember
how we shared the schemes
that used to float with it.

Sometimes a watercolour sun will wash
a blush across the red bricks opposite, illuminate
the blue-black cloud that looms behind;
the light will penetrate that corner of my mind
in which we share all time
in a moment.

One day, maybe, I'll rest
my forearms on the green-painted iron
of Marine Drive's balustrade, watch
for supertankers ghosting the horizon
or wispy sand trails driven by the fishy breeze;
I'll listen to the single roar of a thousand
waves along the shoreline, hear
each voice's own distinctive
ripple, crash or sibilant surrender
in a constant choral exhalation
of your name.

Whenever I caress the hardened heart
carved in the bark of that lofty beech –
or cradle indecisions in the haven
of a hallowed oak – and eavesdrop
on the sounds of things that fall
or grow as the planet breathes
through the trees' tallest fingertips,
then I'll speak in whispers,
just out-loud enough for you to hear.

Another time may be beside
a trig point where the clouds drift
by at eye level, when the wind tugs
at hair: each word ripped
from the page and shouted
will be swept across the dale
to where your ear will be cocked
with a cupped hand behind to catch
every syllable.

Time has no meaning: impressions last;
our future is imbued with all that's passed
between us;
moments we treasured there and then
are here and now,
are always.

Scene 2:   Conflict

Phil Connolly
An Apprentice

strolls up late for their break with the tradesmen's teas,
muddles their measures of sugar and milk.
The foreman sends him for sky nails,
then again for a long stand.
He comes back each time smartly,
empty-handed, with a lot to say.
So they truss his wrists behind his back,
fetter his ankles, gaffer tape
his screams to a purple squeak,
carefully remove his glasses,
place him, face first, in the coffin he's been learning on,
screw down the top,
hoist him on a flatbed truck,
drive him to the cemetery – the fresh-dug grave.
A priest intones as they lower him in.
Shovels deafen him with earth.
The noise of their leaving dies away.
The sounds of his life are his heels
and the back of his head as they flail at the lid.
The sum of his life is the length,
times the width, times the infinite depth
of the absolute, absolute dark.
The time of his life is the runaway hearse
of his heart in his chest and his ears and his mouth...

Peter Wright
Marston Moor

No choice for this family.
Rupert's horsemen had flattened the wheat,
Ironsides taken the oats for livery,
pigs and poultry all lost,
if they wanted to see next winter through
they must cart and bury, dig fast.

God had been everywhere: quite certain
of his Divine Right, the king;
with fire in his belly, the puritan.
Now five thousand lay strewn
thick as sheaves, dismembered,
ridden down, unknown,

Rufforth and Long Marston's quota –
the poor "on the parish", the odd
case who had proved too eager
to serve his conscience. Most now lay
feeding foxes, crows, magpies
in the flyblown heat of early July.

Out in the Ainsty, history had shown
(at Towton, the Pilgrimage of Grace)
that it paid to keep your head down,
not too much passion, sway with the breeze,
lie low, then when the slaughter's done
you may survive on a grave-digger's fees.

*In the village of Rufforth, a square bordered with ancient yews and on former glebe
land, is reputed to be a mass grave where the village dead and other unidentifiable
remains were interred after the battle on 2nd July 1644.*

Frank Broughton
"Ici Donne du Sang"

We could not stop long on the narrow lane
between the wide fields of green corn,
just time for me to frame the unassuming
clump of farmsteads, white walls, tiled roofs,
church spire, the distant mark that all
of you were heading for, then turn and
click again, facing the gentle swell of chalk
you had to cross, you and your pals,
stumbling across the skyline, a perfect target
for the Spandaus stammering in enfilade.
Somewhere on that slope you failed
to ford the hissing stream of lead,
orders said, no stopping for the wounded
so you had to crawl back to our lines
made it, survived, woke up in Blighty
at the end of your one and only trip abroad.
We drive on. At the next village, by the roadside
there's a sign: "Ici Donne du Sang." You did.

Charles Tomson
Wasteland

Pass through the territory
light-footed
and quickly – for

in this wasteland
of dire certainties
is found the lie.

Here ancestral gods
are stripped and
put to the yoke.

You will be offered bribes
but do not succumb,
don't look back.

And if you wonder,
'Why be aware?
Why so? Why so?'

Ask the Jews of Sobibor
the inmates of the camps,
dead children of the snow.

Phil Connolly
The Shanks

Dull blues and greys efface the orange glow;
the stars that never do amount to much.
Stiff back-hands and steel-toed boots,
thuggishly gusting breezes cuff and kick
around dead *Carlsberg* cans, panic
the salvias' cultured heads. And the day's
first blackbird pours his sweet adagio
on *Featherlites*, roaches, the coiffured tresses
of a weeping ash, and you, who missed
the night's last bus, snoring still beneath
a washed-out, final-quarter moon.

Dream on, you'll not sleep long
before bright canopies of birdsong
counterpoint the traffic coughing back to life,
before those keepers of the turf arrive,
your stammered who and why of where you are,
before the shanks pronounce. Silvery-
tongued in the sun, they speak of trespass
versus ownership of place; that bloody way they have.

Scene 3:   Life/ Death

Margaret Speak
At the Skip

I am wearing your garnet ring
with its cluster of red cells

but we have let go most of your
favoured jewellery, brooches, rings,

this thin snake of glass beads which hangs
over the edge of the skip

like the other fine tube snaking
into your arm beneath the Elastoplast.

This would have been the arm
I gripped tight through six hours

of the dead time after midnight.
Each time I let go, you raised it

to claw anxiously at the blankets
and an alarm sounded. I wondered

if it was a conscious act, the way
you knew you had not died yet.

There is a woman here, an expert
at sifting. She'd be an asset at Sotheby's,

the speed she can set a value
on a still-ticking clock or rolled up rug.

With a gesture, she lifts from my hands
a basket full of unmatched crockery.

I am denied the satisfaction
of hearing it shatter. She is eyeing

our car, the raised hatchback covering
a miscellany we have chosen to keep.

Seen through her eyes, the curl of her lip,
this hairbrush looks pathetic, missing bristles:

a silver band worn to a slender crescent
round the bone handle. But I feel

your hand gently pressing my head
while you push it briskly through my long hair.

Peter Wright
Fool's Gold

Feathers lying strewn about,
those of a goldfinch,
primaries glinting like ragwort.
Close inspection shows each quill
nipped near its base,
signature of a sparrow-hawk's bill.
Among thistles, the severed head
minutely, densely feathered,
its front scarlet as arterial blood.

Chill, dull, the sky flat ash-grey
twig and leaf beaded with dew,
the kind of uncommitted day
that might crack with sun-shaft,
paint a pastiche of summer,
overlook the barometer's swift
decline, gales in Fisher, German Bight,
everywhere a battening down,
incorrigible shrinkage of daylight,

and, still wide-eyed, that finch's head,
tree top watchful, timorous, dead.

Charles Tomson
Pilate

Procurator Pilate steps out
across his shining stage
and graciously takes his seat.
Now a flame burns under him
slowly chafing
his softening buttocks.
No bowl of water
or dry Sicilian wine
will put it out.

"Who do you claim to be?"
he finally asks, fumbling
into planetary depths.
His eye-pit slides
through the morning flare
along the floor's mosaic,
looking for the key
to some illusion, some trick
of parallax.

Margaret Speak

Trying Not To Remember a Pink and White Tricycle

We had spread maps across the parquet
trying to find our bearings.
On the scale of difficulty, this must be eleven,
you say. I nod and pick out imaginary specks
on the rug. It is that time of year
when the geese fly overhead in a broad Vee,
honking enough to alert the cat. She stands
on two legs, face pressed to the window pane.
With their passing, grows bored and jumps
into the heap of contours and symbols.
We have no idea of place. Suddenly, I say,
Let Mitzi choose. Somewhere in the circle
where she sits, the point nearest the centre.

                    *   *   *

The box we collect is white, unremittingly ordinary.
It looks lost in the space of the back seat,
so I nurse its lightness, its lack of weight.
We stop once to pick up flowers and candles.
I study the maps. I love them, their crinkled thicknesses,
the impossibility of refolding the original crease,
their colours, the eucalyptus and salmon tints,
the way my finger is drawn along the contours.
But, maps do not look like it is.

                    *   *   *

The box opens easily, the container inside
has a coppery sheen, like the leaves with sun.
We link hands around its circumference.
You concentrate hard on twisting the top,
your tongue between your teeth.
You spiral it high like an American pass,
your eyes closed, but I see
in that arc of ash released
all those absences: no gate,
no blonde plaits with tartan bows,
no tricycle, an Omega where my mouth should be.
I hear between the cries of geese, her voice,
hanging like cut ribbons from the branches.

Scene 4:   Society

Phil Connolly
Part of the Trip

From the time of your life
when your notions of home
were a whiffy suspicion
of urine and damp in the truculent lift,
or a serious, spiralling climb
to the fortnightly three o'clock roar
of a crowd that remained on its feet,
and a set of dependable views:
terraces wove their slate-grey tributaries
south to greet a Thames too sunk
between its banks, too far removed to see,
as vague as mud, but understood,
the seasons' familiar flux in the gardens and park,
bottom left, the Ashkenazis' monumental crush,
the school going nowhere, directly below,
up here in the sky, the sixth-floor flat
two daughters thought a room too small,
the stairs your husband found a step too high,

to the crashing of dawn,
the instant you open your eyes on a fremd light,
your lips to the first of a new day's
umpteen whos and wheres, whens and whys,
your blue tremendous glasses
and, buttressing an ear, the sturdy obsolescence
of your hearing aid; its fading pink.

Frank Broughton
The Inspector of Nuisances' Journal *

This, sir, is my official record.
Twenty years' worth. When not
In use it's under lock and key.
You will appreciate I'm sure

The need for privacy, and precision,
Notes clear and timely. Dates, names,
Address, all other pertinent detail.
Two types of case are listed here,

First what we document as Notifiable
 Disease: diphtheria, scarlet fever, smallpox
 And TB. As for these of course,
Treatment and patient care is no concern

 Of mine. My remit is detergence, scrubbing
And fumigation of premises, bedding,
Privies, sinks, household effects of every kind.
Laborious but essential sir, I like to think.

Then secondly, complaints, which tend
You'll find if you scan down this page
To be repetitive in nature, improper
Keeping of pigs, overlarge deposits

Of dung in yards, You've spotted something
Odd? Horse slaughtering in the wrong place?
(The inn stables sir, next to the Wesleyans,
I'll leave the rest to your imagination).

The last two columns "Actions "and "Results"
Are where, if I may stoop to the vernacular, I earn
My corn, official letter or a quiet word, which
To employ, a matter of experience I'd say,

But note the final column, every box confirms
"Attended to" or "satisfactory" The red dot?
Denotes fatality, that one is scarlet fever, you'll
Know I'm sure the row of cottages on the Wynd?

A boy of seven as I remember it
But marked as satisfactory? Correct
Prompt disinfection and a thorough
Fumigation, after the event.

*Journal and Continuous Record of the Inspector of Nuisances
(on display in the town museum, Richmond, North Yorkshire)

Debbie Jayne Howell
York Real Ale Festival

The bar staff in fur boots and eyeliner
only take cash
this isn't a place for women's talk.
Warm lines croon in wall masonry.
Two pence pieces propping up the iron legs
of the gnarled wooden table.

A music of sorts jars the sports commentary
from the TV, as you multi-task and work out Sudoku,
talk to the throng gathering to stare and shout
at the dots on screen, remembering.
Conversations on Chamberlain – is he dead?
Politics for sports watchers.

Saturday afternoon rain then hail
and more arrive to prop up the bar,
more beer ordered.
The festival has hardly started.
28 cask beers – how many can be drunk
before falling over and appealing to the wife.

There is comfort in the noise of alone.
The weight of the world lifts;
an iron bar of bad banks,
people quivering in money corners
kept somewhere else.
Singing World Cup songs –

'If it's Wednesday it must be Wembley'
by the Thomson Twins.
Hailing outside again very dark for light,
move to talk of Dave Clark Five.
"Nil: nil" on television
not sure of the teams.
Just the sound of your voice reading the
Finance page looking up from time to time to
review strategy and agree with banter.
Life still happens; same talk, different people
from age to age,
another afternoon, more rain.

Peter R White

Perambulations

Each time I walk the dog, it's time alone:
I seize the chance and use the only way
we have to keep in touch – I use my phone.

Each trip's a verbal tryst as, unbeknown
to them, we have liaisons twice a day,
each time I walk the dog; it's time alone,

with mobile at my ear, all reason thrown
in turmoil by this reckless interplay
we have. To keep in touch, I use my phone

for furtive dialogues; his soothing tone,
like fingers down my spine, makes senses sway
each time.   I walk the dog: it's time alone

for stolen moments with that special one
whose love has put my world in disarray.
We have to keep in touch – I use my phone

because I'm sure my children would disown
me if they knew the games I play
each time I walk the dog. It's time alone
we have. To keep in touch, I use my phone.

Scene 5:   Place

Frank Broughton
Night on the Prairie

1885

These shining constellations seem
less distant than the hissing lamps
of Boston, Chicago, Kansas, cities
she passed through in a dream

on the hard road west, to lie
 unsleeping in this hut he built of
 sod and sweat, lodged in the very
core of emptiness, where every

signpost (if there were signposts here)
would point north, south, east, west
to the same five hundred rolling miles
of nothing but prairie grasses constantly

whispering *What drove you to this place?*
 What love? What hate? What fear?
 Questions floating in the air
 like seeds, like the fine dust

that sifts through shutters, doors,
a drifting, grey, unending snow,
as prairie wolves howl
under the high, cold stars.

1895

When the moon is full
I watch its pale glow paint
a false dawn on the blind.
He snores beside me, his
arm heavy across my breast,
his breathing quick and rough.

I try to remember how it was
I came to lie here, listening
to the night winds whining
through the stove, wondering
how it is I am sharing his bed,
missing yours.

He is not even a moon to your sun,
he is cloud, dull, grey with rain.
I wish that your fierce rays
would burn him off or I could
become the wind, drive him far
beyond the horizon.

1931

A billion, billion grains of sand give
muscle to the mountain wind, a gritty,
choking night erases sun, moon, stars.

Their land is taking flight, heading
for Missouri, Arkansas, nothing left
to root in until they too are blown away,

blown to the bright land of apples big as pumpkins,
movie goddesses and gods they worshipped
at the picture house in Wichita.

What's left? A sun-scorched empty shack,
a mile of rusty barbs, a cast-iron stove,
one load too many for their worn-out Ford.

1985

Glaring galaxies of light advance,
a phalanx, disciplined as machines
built to make war not bread.

This lumbering apocalypse of noise
 consumes the standing wheat
in roaring celebration of the death

of what bloomed here before the plough:
prairie rose, paintbrush, bluestem,
purpletop, wild rye and shooting star,

And those who first set steel into this earth?
Their loves and hates, their hopes and fears
are buried deeper than the poisoned flowers.

John Atkinson
Harvest Light

spilled like grains of time across remembered lands,
drove mist and dew from the straw-covered
and thirst-cracked earth:

a combine's broad mouth waiting by a field's edge
on coming warmth to dry the ripened corn,
bread or beer from the giving ground;

the sacks in the barn, a regiment of sagging bellies
stacked two high on the grit-stone slabs
of the old threshing floor;

the smell of wheat and jute, the sun, raying through
slits in stone walls, dust, shining like stars
swirled in Brownian motion,

solar systems disturbed by swallows flashing under
lofty beams, to light on bowls of daubed clay
brimming with hungry beaks.

How many recall bagging corn; the harvest's weight
poured into cargoes of gold, and drinkin's
in a wicker basket: white pint mugs,

corned beef sandwiches, a gallon of strong tea, warm
from the chipped enamel urn? Sweet rest
for weary backs in August heat.

Debbie Jayne Howell
Silence and Sounds

You were out at the barber's, trying to manage
your steely grey and the workmen that had plagued
all week were taking a break, so the blackbird's
four ascending notes could be heard again.

Purple lavender and orange poppies not yet in
bloom, were not enough to tempt the courtyard bees,
who were gone or dead; buzzing a pneumatic drill
unwillingly breaking road a thousand ways.

You appear at the door shorn, frowning, rattled by noise.
The terrified cat slinks out a welcome, returns under the
bed, his blacked out eyes plead a temporary truce.
Time for wine to hide frustration, soak up and distract.

You whistle tunelessly preparing food in the kitchen.
The screeches from the lorries dissipate,
voices too, tarmac renewed is left to set.
More gas mains to work on in another street.

The cat appears, settles on the cushion and
with a deep sigh, rearranges paws and sleeps.
Sun spills out like saved cream, kept for a treat.
A yellow-blue opulence that fills every corner.

Warm breezes rustle the ivy in the courtyard
and the Japanese wind chimes begin to tinkle.
You turn me from behind; begin to kiss me
and silence softly led becomes a different sound.

Jamie Howell
The Courtyard

There are different ages of brick
pock-marked with the choke of industry;
designer-living in an obituary of black,
backyard glass reflecting the closed-off concerns
of others since Victoriana -
that 'Please sir, I want more' request.
The quiet buzz of the bees soothes
in the salsa of sky, purple on blue,
lavender scent stealing the breeze.
Herbal infusions lose themselves in thyme
Tarragon, camomile, parsley and mint
mix calypso cocktails in the language of the city;
a cauldron on the rooftops
amongst the salvia vermilion red.

Margaret Speak
The Small canvas

There is light angled
through an attic casement.
It falls geometrically
on the desk in its narrow alcove
on the slanted mirror.

Twin pencils of light
point to an open fan
with its Japanese inks
and pale pagodas.

A friend visited this room,
said it remained exactly so
but the painter was missing.

Though her palettes remained
the titanium white had crusted,
looked silver and grey
like snow at the edge
of an arterial road.

Scene 6:   Philosophy

Charles Tomson
Lucifer

A toast to m'self
if that's not immodest,
to the finger on the string,
to the scarlet brush-tip
poised before its canvas,

to the bat that flies
along the molten filaments
of the brain, the spirit-bird
circling the glowing deep.

My stinger pierces to the ganglion.
My peregrine stoops its prey.
My gunner's rammer plunges
down the barrel. I hold the
smoking tow that lights the charge.

I am the drum, tapping
through the frosted ranks
across the naked cornfields,
the crested bugle call at dawn.

Debbie Jayne Howell
Warkworth Beach

Shift colours of sun
bounce aqua a dark green
brown to shore.

Where creamy white
tide lines
hide mortality.

Blue to type
pushes away cloud,
murmurs to shade.

Garrulous people fade
in a roar of surf
joy surged.

Tansy yellow sand dunes
feel sand grains
sting in glint gold.

Difficult to see
across the light;
sea sand brings shells

drift wood and pebbles in;
solace immeasurable.
Our time here is temporal.

Peter R White
Karma

Everything I see
will alter me
ever so slightly.

Each thought that enters
my subconscious
or my conscience
will make a vague amendment
to who I am.

Each imposition of my human right,
my every heartbeat's energy will interfere
with the environment;
each breath will modify the atmosphere
we share.

Each trace of joy or fear,
each act of diligence
or self indulgence
will affect the aura I transmit
to those around me,
encourage them to make their own,
ever so slight
additions or subtractions
to or from the blend.

Each time I smile or sound
an angry horn
I will engender empathy
or scorn
within the global ambience.

Every word I write or utter,
every tacit nod or shake in silence
matters, makes a difference,
modifies our co-existence.

My slight significance
imposes great responsibility.

Jamie Howell
Shorelines

walk across a cubist insight
grey white gold

the old minimal is me
outside all three

the winds steel heartbeat
sharp to shore

ozone lays
that maul me

desired
mer d'embrace

tortured rills
writhe

reach for
dragged back screaming

nail and hair torn
seabirds pick the ruin

sing lament
feed on lonely

stand here a thousand years
happy dead

run and run and run
till breathless fallen

one with myself
in hymnal praise

between all three
now three in one

no longer lonely
free

John Atkinson
Attempted Landscapes

There was in the beginning one sole Self; no eye winked.
He thought: ' Shall I create territories?' (Aitareya-Upanishad)

First paint a mountain or two, a small range capped with snow,
and to rescue it from an excess of white let the slopes tumble
into a wooded valley with a torrent of foaming melt-water
hurtling over boulders, framed by deciduous – no coniferous ...

On second thoughts begin again; with rolling hills, fading
one after the other into the horizon. This seems a better start.
Now for some trees; I imagine a forest, not overdone,
    spreading
to the far right of the canvas. Centre left a crescent bay, edged

by waves breaking on the sand and cupped by cliffs that face
a sea loosing itself at the edge of the sky. A glistening surface
reflects an ochre-red sun, a tongue of dappled gold, glowing
beneath crimson flame-tinged clouds, fringed by ...

I wonder, am I really up to this? Maybe my modest artistic
ability points to a need for more practice, acute observation;
to master my art, or live in hope the world may reshape itself
into a subject easier to paint. Of course I could try abstraction.

No – one more attempt; abandon the sea and turn the forest
into a wood. Lift the sun higher, try to capture the feeling
of warmth in its light. I need water, so in the middle ground
a river running through, edged by meadows of wild flowers,

as if stirred by gentle breezes: reed mace surrounding pools,
willow, oak, scattered cattle, a thatched croft of pale stone.
Also I need people, not many, and distant, involved in pastoral
labours – Arcadian. Now I'm nearly done. But perhaps

one more thing, in the near ground a figure advancing. A rustic
man broadcasting seed on a field of flinty earth. And when I
have used all my palette and skill to paint away his sins it will
be perfect, leaving nothing between the viewer and the view.

Scene 7:   Faith

Margaret Speak
Noah's Wife

He chose Gopher trees,
branding his initial
huge as a fist
into the bark.
Excited, we lay beneath
their dense canopy,
squinted at sunlight,
soaked up their resin.

Night after night
he worked the wood,
sawing the planks,
whittling the pegs,
driving me distracted
to my cousin's tent;
we shared her hearth.
He built his boat
(sweet as honey to him)
counted the cubits.
Our sons helped him
spread the pitch.
Each measured a ladder
for the second, third
and lower decks.
We waited for the rains.

They came, seeped damp
into our garments, sandals,
sacks of salt and debelah.
We climbed aboard
with a pair of oxen,
a couple of lambs,
many more, (he left nothing behind)
barley, wine, the finest oil;
many days to prepare
and soon to sail.
My sadness lifts like a cloud
under the roof of the ark
as just one flicker of sun
shows clear the shadow of his
letter *N* pale as olives.

Charles Tomson

Epiphany

Some say they are kings
who hazard this winter journey
bearing tributes for a child.
A romance in the old sense
their names colour the allusions.
What did they come to see?
A babe wrapt in the stars.

A legend themselves
they crowd the house
with gifts of what lies ahead.
A goat bleats from a dark corner;
its trough is, for a while, a throne.
Do not touch, do not finger them.
They dissolve in the sweat of your hand.

Phil Connolly
Right at the Crux

Bright at their backs, sunlight shafting Christ,
hosts of angels, and whatever their collective nouns,
countless sinners and saints, variegates indoors,
spangles heads and shoulders, shirts and frocks.

The crowd that stuffs the nave this clammy mass
breathes in and out, devours its oxygen, inflates
its heat, prepares the stage for me, my party piece.
Just as the priest lifts the Body of Christ to his lips,

I faint. Slumped in my pew, utterly relaxed,
my nasal tract, my bladder drop their guard.
Minutes pass. Pale as ash, I snort myself awake,
blush to the roots of my father's shame.

Once more disgraced among the icons,
I catch the Virgin's eye. I sense her empathy.
She turns away. I must be wrong.
The gaudy claustrophobia... the droning on...

Frank Broughton
A Life in the Circus

My grandfather pedalled a unicycle
simultaneously juggling
half a dozen plates.
The clowns chased him
but he never fell off.

My father rode a pony bareback
while eating fire, then swallowed
a sword for dessert.
A tiger escaped and pursued him,
still he remained unflustered
and to frantic applause,
clung to his seat, taming the beast
by force of personality.

Keen to follow in their footsteps
I attempted a high wire act.
Sadly, vertigo overcame ambition,
I plunged 50 feet but had the luck
to break my fall
on a large lady in the front row
(she was given CPR and a full refund).

I decided on a change of direction
and now partner Noona,
the Navajo Knifethrower.
All I have to do is to shut my eyes,
keep still and avoid any derogatory
references to Native Americans.
It's a living, so far.

Phil Connolly
The Deal

Sunday, and I'm dreading mass so much
I find myself beseeching God to put me out.
I don't mean cast, as in adrift – lose me

in a wilderness, or have me dumped:
illicit tipping in some cul-de-sac.
Just intercede on my behalf,

spare me the marathon's Latin drag,
seal me this pact with Father Finn:
he'll hypnotize me on the starting line,

I'll sleep-walk all the stand and chant,
sit, not fidget, pay attention, kneel
and echo-mumble *kyrie eleison*

in an incense-drench of rigmarole and retribution,
while he prays for my immortal soul.
And when the wine runs out, he'll snap

his fingers, blink me back to here and now,
intone the code for time to leave,
pass God's blessing on, and let me go.

Scene 8:   Intrigue

Peter Wright
Lost at Sea

Shunning the fulsome words of public plaques
she stands before redundant simple things:
coat-hooks, a shaving mirror, that spare key.

Never one for school, he'd bunked off,
faced uproar when he asked
what use is maths or history to me?

Already his mind was miles away
baiting lethal hooks alongside uncles, cousins
far removed, cresting a turbulent sea.

So that night when the roar rose
to hurricane force and waves made black
mountains over the masts, did he

pause in the seconds when all fight was gone
to hear stern words from school or kirk?
Or did a fleeting sense of continuity

provide his shroud when, heavy as an otterboard
he was engulfed by the element which
from childhood had absorbed his energy?

Margaret Speak
Vivaldi's bow

I've begun to finger the bow
and imagine those melancholy sighs
which trembled from his lips
on freezing Thursdays in the orphanage.

He had the patience of a cat,
the temper of a wild wind coming up the canal.
He hated most of us but sometimes his head
would be still beneath his red strands of hair.

Once I saw him pluck a swatch, thread it between
the usual horsehair, play a riff, the scales.
We would play as he stalked the rows,
stopped near a girl: she would tremble at her violin.

He'd begin scribbling a piece just for her,
for the next concert. I'd feel nauseous
because it wasn't me. My playing didn't excite
though I practised to exhaustion.

There was a turning over of the place
when the bow went missing.
I slipped it into the gap under the marble step
as I scrubbed it with my raw hands.

This my daily chore: my red hands were never
for coaxing true music out of maplewood
and spruce but they could clean and polish
marble fit for Vivaldi's shoes.

Jamie Howell
Prospero's Kiss

Sheer the shadows
eat the ends of verse.
Night resplendent,
storm sparks of black
contrive to make the dawn
a masque,
a starlit paper haze
dances, in a lunar gaze of pain.
(Convolutions)

Intense desire betrayed
cross the 'T's and vitriol all 'I's.
Caliban regis to a bidden word,
flaws all majesty
and lost to slavery lays trial,
tribulation to Ariel's dungeon dreams,
in forms unseen,
thus,
all hope condemned
within the magician's wish
in paths lain wracked
and ship-wreck hidden.

Day gives birth to other shadows.
Old age groans in grey reflect we sky,
in shades that wish for
necromance the cats grey-hame
and silhouettes, soprano sing
conspire for better times
than this in Prospero's sad kiss.

All magic put aside
the mage of different ends
portends a broken staff,
happiness lost and found,
potent words in ashes beaten black
into the ground.
Foment a happy end?
Should we pretend or audience each
other's slavery as foe or friend;
suspend all disbelief.

Frank Broughton
Hansel and Gretel make it big

"Come in my dears, you're soaking wet!
Take off your boots, here, let me
place them by the fire and hang
your cloaks up on the drier. Quick,
 strip your clothes, they're sodden too,
your toes and fingers look quite blue.
I've soft, dry towels to wrap you in
and rub the life back to your skins.
Now here's a treat, my special brew
of herbs and spice to warm you through.
Make sure you drink up every drop,
You're feeling sleepy? Flop
on this couch and have a snooze
while I just pop next door and choose
the perfect size of baking tin
to fit two chubby children in
and check Nigella's latest book
for her advice on how to cook
them to a turn, all sweet and tender.
Or should I pop them in the blender?"

But sadly for the witch's plan
before she'd found the ideal pan
to roast them in, the cunning two
(who'd poured her potions down the loo)
crept up behind the evil crone
and wacked her with the heavy stone
she used to keep her door ajar
then (maybe this was going too far)

they dragged her back across the floor
and shoved her through the oven door
giving a merry shout of glee
as they set the dial to "Gas Mark 3."
And so the witch's plan misfired
and our two kids were quickly hired
to host a new show on TV
replacement for "Come Dine With me"
which led these infant cannibals
to star in Heston Blumenthal's
new primetime evening cookery slot
"You'll Never Guess What's in my Pot!"

Debbie Jayne Howell
Brief Encounter at Bristol

It rained as we walked to Brunel's great vessel,
our smiles infectious as the world engineered
rainbows and hopeful definitions.

The seductive posters had changed
at Temple Meads Station,
walls now blank, untidy and dull.
Photographs you wanted to take
of the blond in the grey clinging dress;
the man in glasses, with eyes only for her

where his hand wandered from her upper
spine to the lower curve of her buttocks;
rubbing, caressing, but never still.

She wriggled against him to stop, yet
leaned more urgently against the brick,
her whole being in perfect union with his.

We sat watching them from the other platform
Vettriano like, talking of an imaginary
poster of a cigarette in someone's mouth

as you moved your hand along my arm.
We were voyeurs you and I that day
did we want to join in, be watched ourselves?

Scene 9: Love/romance

Jamie Howell
Yet

I have no wings so I can't fly,
yet,
I dream in blue and float as clouds
in all my thoughts of you.

I have no scaled flanks to course the sea,
yet,
I feel the storm scald the surf
in visions borne of you.

I have no roots, dig in rock laid bare,
yet,
delve the earth in whispers,
rumours of the beauty that is you.

I have an ember glowing bright,
yet,
a fiery tempest eating all the world
illuming all of me, a star in darkness,
that my love, is you.

Peter R White
Aberford Blues

No wandering cloud felt lonelier than I,
nor turned a cornflower sky such dismal grey
as when bright talk of spring finds no reply;
this conversation only flows one way.

Still kestrels hover, kites and buzzards soar;
beech is still bare, but willow's in display;
bluebells and garlic groves still wait to flower.
I am unmoved: you are not here today.

There was a time when exercise was all –
when mileage clocked and stamina and speed
were what I valued when I heard the call
to walk – but now I feel a different need:

I simply want you there to answer back,
for there is nothing I would rather do
than amble onto any rustic track
to walk and talk a mile or two with you.

Debbie Jayne Howell
Kimono Calligraphy

The couple on the train dress as Europeans;
make a percolated sound not realized in English.
She moves closer and smiles a thousand words:
'Does the wind move or is the heart restless?'
Her jet-black hair shines as it falls against him,
fuses kimono colour rich in orange blossom
from the silk scarf he holds in place.
Her ancient voice takes the present away,
folds the paper that makes the red lanterns
and inks the series of symbols on the white wall;
infinity brushes higher red on black;
the symbol for rain locks a prisoner's window
the tree enquires skirt like, sensitive and female
conjures memory only they know and remember.

Phil Connolly
Where's Vic?

I used to pause the news, put down my book,
reduce the heat – delay our Sunday roast, defer
a shopping trip, whatever; go and sit beside her,
warm her hands in mine, trust in time's desire
to heal – the palliative of fourteen years
and, tenderly of course, repeat myself
in three brief words, the last of which was Mum.

But the whites of her eyes ballooned and froze,
the way a rabbit petrifies in halogen.
And the tremulous O of her lips was the mouth
of the pit where the shock of her life crashed in.
These every time she has to know I say
he's just popped out to buy some cigarettes
and any second he'll come waltzing in that door.

Jamie Howell

The Poet's Burden and The Husband's Hope

If there is love beyond the grave
then we will meet
and dance in all our memories (complete)
our bodies in their twilight heat
shall fire our souls.

If beyond that furthest shore
there are no lovers (arms)
in which to rest
and all in shade and shadow
lays all we are to dust
in hell and nothing,
then, everything I write,
mere poor reflections,
shall nonetheless count us now as blessed.

If, beyond the grave we meet
there is no love
then everything I write
shall cast its spell
turn back time and space until it cracks,
pours all hope upon, till then a barren floor.
In that dark
I'll build a door...
to you
and in that light ajar we'll stand renewed...
beyond, my love,
that farthest shore.

Scene 10:   Nature

John Atkinson
Lepus Becoming

The Glory that was Rome marched north and westward,
boarding boats to reach these shores. The legions carried
carnage, death and a living larder of rabbits and snails;
also an idea there was one God only, to rule over Heaven
and Earth – but he did have a son. Hare, on the other hand,
arrived before the North Sea gave rise to shores, or a need
for boats, so he ambled and galloped across the lost land
from God knows where. Then, famously moon-struck, he
becomes the favourite of Eostre, and who can blame her?

Beneath the face of the paschal moon he tries to forget
his sorrows: the rabbits, who – like Romans, tolerate
no competition – kill and eat the brains of his young,
then the followers of God's son, equally multiplying;
steal his mistress's birthday to fix a singular death.

        *   *   *

The swish of keen scythes could be heard when man
followed man, cutting swathes in successive arcs,
each described by the snaith's wooden curves, bent
through three dimensions: and gritty against a blade's
peened edge, the rub of carbide stones, tapered ends
wearing away in the mowers' measured strokes. Once
their grating tones scraped across the fields of England.

Later the clatter-clat song of a reaper's cutter-bar,
then the thrum of the combine's deafening drum.
All have sung round and round falling stands of corn
where shapes of men waited with sticks and guns.

A nose twitches to windward, concealed ears cower,
prick up to listen; monocular vision hunts for humans.
Soon my friend your time to run will come.

*   *   *

Owd Sally, Grimalkin, Moll, Mawkin, Jack-o'-the-stubble
Furze-cat, Swift-as-wind; there are places where his name
is not spoken should it bring ill luck to those whose auguries
place him badly. Orion would invoke him, invite him
to the hunt, to race against dogs; outwit them if he can.
He'll make a maze of his own scent with turns and sweeps:
retrace steps, jump walls, dykes, hide in flocks of sheep
until the dogs have lost him. Chased and chasing across
the meat-eating Earth, a great heart pumps to arteries,
muscle and lungs. But he must tire, and when he does
fetch the cooking pot, build a fire to roast his flesh,
mix blood with wine; after this feast he will become man.

If there is a familiar to guide us toward our end I would like
mine to be hare, running with me, leaping between worlds.

Peter Wright
Spring Water

Four attempts to soft-shoe somewhere near
where they doze on the farther reaches
of the beck, heads tucked but so wary
that the dog's bobbing always springs
them at three hundred paces
in tight formation, dipping, swervy.

Stealth at last reveals the drake's
grey speckle, chestnut, bottle-green, cream
tending to apricot; plumage to beguile,
to captivate his dusky lover.
As they fly their softly whistled calls
blow the secret of their name: teal, teal.

Water, amber, placid as a mirror
then fretted by a gusty breeze
for this is April, whose urgent songs
insist that love is in the air.
The rudd seek shadow under trees
where skeins of pondweed flow like green hair

and the balloon snagged on a branch
offers some hastily scribbled thoughts
now besmirched on its torn silver,
sentiments that must have seemed brave,
words like yours and forever
bleached under new light, rinsed by wave.

John Atkinson
Casual Sex

The power of population is indefinitely greater than
the power of the earth to produce subsistence to man.
(Thomas Malthus 1766 – 1834)

Winter's dressed to leave, spring dips a toe
to test the water, gives the go ahead
for frogs to come hopping, flopping in
from all around. At times ponderous – a suitable attitude
for a pond – with the perfect breast-stroke
and a chirruping love-song to entrance a mate.
Vacant eyeballs blink, little distortions in the meniscus,
more underwater; like adolescent lovers who fidget
on muddy sofas, wish lingering parents off to bed.
Grey gobs of spotty jelly smother the shallows;
overnight the frogs depart, free of care
for their offspring's fate. But some will survive;
only a few considering the multitude spawned,
when they burgeoned in margins, rasping at algae,
a writhing mass of soot-coloured mallard fodder.

Compare and contrast to the human predicament:
top predator, survival potential excellent,
a unique ability to contemplate future demise;
yet powerless to do anything about it. And stalked
by a prurient hunger as though it were an Other.

Nine thousand an hour, a hundred thousand by morning,
one and a half million next week,
a billion.

Peter R White
To be is to intrude

This tree was old before my father
met my mother; a tree which
in sapling its own way will still spill
keys after my white bones
have turned to ash.
I want:

to be
in a place, off path
so deep that life's erosion
by humanity
is baffled by the wild tranquillity
of trees, where boughs that fall are left
to enhance moss and ants;

to scuttle
gravity-free
with a nuthatch, experience
the fineness of its feathers,
hack at hazelnuts;

to spawn
the musk of fungi, emit
essences of garlic;

to belong
to the bloom
of bluebells, blend
into spaces where a deer

or a hare may nibble, creep,
listen to the leaves;

not as an observer, an exploiter
of the experience. I need to feel
included.

Margaret Speak
The Last of the Reindeer Riders

THE WOMAN

The deer were her diary:
she wrote her thoughts on their skins,
traced ideas along their antlers.
What she remembered of Ulan Bator;
the university, translating to Russian
but missing Hovsgol,
the white beauty of winter
battling the ice,
the long thaw into spring.
She had come home in summer
heavy with longing and child
and stayed.

Now, three children, no Russian.
The circle of work repeated,
pleases her, sends her tired to her bed.
Sometimes she plays
makes a picture of her name,
Tsetge, a flower of moss,
lichen, mushrooms, but the deer
come and eat, nibbling at the heart.
They pay her well:
this one the best milker
this one the tastiest cheese
this one the creamy yoghurt.
And when they run
are a sea of white silk
rippling downhill.

THE BRIDE

What can I tell you?
They sent us
hands tied back to back
seated on reindeer
down to the winter pasture
to be alone
until next new moon.
our saddlebags were packed
with cheese, yoghurt, bread.
A gentle ride
but the fear inside me
is a flighting of reindeer.

In the forest
we stop and he unties
those bonds, but rubbing my wrists
he is making more.
I see stars stitched
in the charcoal gauze
of the night sky
while we were sucked
deep into the black earth.
We make soft indentations
in the silvered green:
the leaves above
are a sorcerer's knot.

I tell you how I feel:
I will scoop up those stars
from the surface of the lake:
give them to him, a promise
next Spring, a son
his first steps clumsy,
wobbly-legged as new-born deer;
he will track their spoor.

THE HUNTER

I like the early morning light
white and fragile as snowdrops.
The reindeer lifts his hooves:
I warm my hands in his steaming breath
sit astride his reluctant back
feet planted in the river.
So! I spear salmon and trout
with my trident,
the metal beaten like fishscales.
Sometimes a hunting trip
is as long as seven dawns:
with my larchwood horn
I imitate wild deer
stalk him, he is tame for me.
Once I cradled an eagle.
The wash of winter rivers
echoes round our tight space.
I love Hovsgol even then.
always the herding of reindeer;

swollen with pleasure
we expand in summer pastures.
This year my seed inside my woman,
my son will be born with reindeer babies in spring.
And when life is hard
vodka makes me brave.

THE SHAMAN

My bones flaky as ash
I play dead
even my skin does not breathe.

Inside my head
spirals of light, shrill voices
summon my guardian spirit.

The tremble begins
words spew from my mouth
I take up my drum.

There is thunder and rage
in my hands;
the moon is aflame.

My people chant;
Gambuxu, Gambuxu.
We are swaying and dancing.

The one with the troubled soul
stands like a weak shadow,
I must entice his soul.

This is the spirit
with ice or a stone
for a heart

evil as a glitter of stars.
The drumming is a rustle
at the edge of the lake.

The lip of the moon
as dense as coral
but my brother is now at peace.

Oh yes, I practise deception
use tricks, magic,
chant my incantations.

I fear for tomorrow:
sometimes a confusion of words
and the spirits do not answer my calls.

Once our people were many
now are as few as the days
between three new moons.

THE CHILD

Covering her slate
with her first careful words
MUMMA and reindeer names
her favourite, SUYAN.
Travelling eight times a year:
always a reindeer back
her fur cradle strapped safe, she counted the stars
or cried herself to sleep
or listened to the Shaman's drum.

Father chopped branches for the yurt:
she striding the spaces
for him to place the poles
and tie the tops into a cone.
She was first to crawl
inside the dark felt
unpack her basket of braids
set out the eagle feather,
coral beads, speckled stone,
made each place home.

She learned to milk the deer
set the best for cheese,
would follow the women
in their search for one
missing from the herd.

She loved best when Gambuxu
called the spirits
in his eagle-feather headdress
drumming up the dead souls,
wearing the colours of hope.

THE PHOTOGRAPHER

We focus them in the distance
and excitement is shuttered inside
viscous as gelatine.
This is my tribe from the Tuva:
the Tsaatang, those with white reindeer.
Thunder as the reindeer speed down
shaking the mountain,
their harness jangling,
the bells ringing like hooves.

Their owners range after;
commanding, cajoling.
Some ride them, proud jockeys,
others have babies tied to their backs.
No curiosity about my camera;
they are used to Gambuxu's tricks.
Mostly they scowl into the sun
dressed bright as a prism of butterflies.

They hold their old German rifles
like children with plastic replicas
ready for hunting, their faces
innocent and curved as fisheye.
Women sew with a needle of bone
embroider caps and braids.
The child copies in anxious stitches
re-threading the small aperture.

They live as their ancestors
adapting to the rhythms of the herd,
the flare of the sun, the filter of snow
summoning monochrome spirits.
as they seek the circle of fire,
withdraw into the warmth of the yurt
my guide pointed to my camera,
asked what I wanted it to show.
I replied, "Their welcome
and the musty aroma of reindeer."

*(The Tsaatang are a nomadic tribe
who live in Mongolia.)*